Dried Flower Arranging

Text and Floral Designs by
MING VEEVERS-CARTER

4449
© 1995 Coombe Books
This edition published in 1995 by Coombe Books
for Parragon Book Service Ltd, Unit 13-17,
Avonbridge Trading Estate, Atlantic Road,
Avonbridge, Bristol BS11 9QD
All rights reserved.
Printed in Hong Kong
ISBN 1-85813-829-9

Photography by
STEVE TANNER

Dried Flower
Arranging

‖ •PARRAGON• ‖

Contents

Introduction

▲ Bunches of colourful Helichrysum being commercially air-dried.

Dried flowers are no longer dull and lifeless winter substitutes for the abundance of fresh flowers available in the spring, summer and autumn. Improved techniques for drying have made commercially-dried flowers vibrant in colour, strong in shape and wide in variety. This high quality dried plant material lends itself to creating truly stunning and unique displays and decorations for the home for long-lasting pleasure, as exemplified by the designs in this book. However, many types of garden flower and foliage can be simply and successfully dried at home, which can be used in conjunction with exotic, commercially-dried items. Woods and waysides offer a rich harvest of cones and nuts, seedheads, pods and fungi for use in arrangements. Even artificial fruits and flowers can be imaginatively combined with natural dried material to produce richly-coloured displays.

Drying Flowers

Air-drying is the easiest and cheapest method of preserving plant material, although some plants are better preserved by using desiccants or glycerine. Plants should be harvested on a dry day after any dew has evaporated. They should be grouped in small bunches, the stems bound together tightly near their bases with an elastic band and hung upside-down in a dry, dark and well-ventilated interior. A boiler, empty airing cupboard, warm attic or over a radiator are all ideal sites. Leave the flowers to dry for several days – the exact length of time will vary according to the type of plant. Check thoroughly to make sure that the flowers

Desiccants – sand, borax or silica gel – draw moisture from plants to preserve them. Silica gel, the most effective and the most expensive desiccant, is available usually in the form of white crystals from chemist shops or hardware stores. The stems of flowers to be dried in this way must be trimmed to 2.5 cm (1in) in length. Carefully cover the flowers with the crystals, inside and around each bloom. When fully covered, replace the lid of the container and store in a warm place for about 48 hours.

are completely dry before use. Make sure hydrangea heads are firm to the touch. These flowers, together with delphiniums, are best dried singly. Always dry more than you need since there will probably be some casualties.

A bunch of roses in their fresh state and after being air-dried. The blooms shrink a good deal but also open out a little after they have been hanging up. The colours have been well-preserved although they do change in hue.

Equipment

Dry florist's foam is generally essential for making dried flower arrangements. There are blocks that can be easily cut and shaped to fit containers; balls of varying sizes which can be used for topiaries (page 48), rose or bay balls (page 34); cones which can also be used for topiaries (page 83) and rings which are used as a base for wreaths (page 32). Nylon-reinforced plaster is ideal for setting trunks in pots when making topiaries. And a glue gun is an excellent tool and can be used to glue all kinds of items onto wreaths, baskets, wood and fabric. There are various thicknesses of florist's wire, but I only use four kinds: 18 and 22 gauge stem wires and narrow and thick silver wire. Stem binding tape has two purposes: it gives an extra hold to wire stems and conceals the wire. Anchor tape is a strong adhesive tape used to secure foam and moss to containers. Green canes are used for making stems longer. Wire-edged ribbon is considerably more expensive than ordinary ribbon but can be moulded into a variety of shapes that will hold.

▲ Choosing your container is as important as selecting your flowers. Its size, shape and texture is important and will dictate to a certain extent the shape of the arrangement. As an approximate guide, the arrangement should be twice the height of the pot and twice the width.

◄ Before embarking on an arrangement collect together the essentials: dried florist foam balls or cones, wire-edged ribbon a glue gun and florist's wires.

▲ Cover a footed bowl by spreading out a piece of fabric right side down and place the pot in the centre. From underneath, gather up the fabric around the bowl's 'neck' and hold in place with one hand. Turn the bowl upside down and secure fabric to neck with a wire. Holding pot around neck, pull fabric downwards gently to make even gathers all the way round. Now turn upright again and tuck excess fabric into the top of the pot.

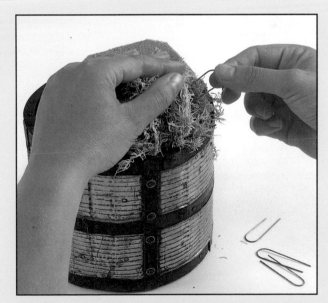

▲ Make pins from 18 or 22 gauge stem wire by cutting into 7.5-10cm (3-4in) lengths and bending in half. Use to pin plastic backing to moss and moss or strings of chillies to foam.

▲ Dry foam fillings are used in shallow bowls, flat dishes or plastic trays. Fill containers with foam to a higher level than their rim. Cover with a little sphagnum moss and secure in place with adhesive tape. For narrow-necked containers, cut the foam a fraction bigger than the neck width and push into the pot.

Techniques

Making Bows

To make a single bow with tails: Make a loop in the ribbon on either side of your thumb and forefinger leaving a similar length of hanging ribbon on either side as tails. Cut ribbon and twist one end of a 22 gauge stem wire around the middle.
Double-looped bow: As above except make 2 loops either side instead of one. To finish bow, cut a small length of ribbon and tie around the middle to cover the wire. Trim off excess ribbon at the bow back.
Single loop without tails: As single bow but do not make tails. Tuck the short ribbon ends into the loops and wire as before.

Fabric bows

Cut a strip of fabric four times the required width and fold in half lengthways. Fold in half again, bringing the raw long edges to meet the fold, and glue. Cut the short ends diagonally, turn under the raw edges and glue. Make a bow with or without tails. To make the 'knot', cut a narrow length of fabric and with the reverse facing, fold the raw long edges into the middle, overlap and glue. Tie around the middle of the bow and cut off excess, or use this to form tails. Use the glue sparingly so that it does not seep through the fabric.

▲ DRY FOAM BLOCK: Cut a piece of wire netting roughly twice the size of the block(s). Line the netting with a thin layer of moss and wrap around the block. Along the length of the block, twist the cut wire ends around the netting to secure. Cut away the excess netting at the sides of the block and twist the cut ends onto the netting.

▲ MOSS ROPE: Cut a strip of wire netting 20cm (8in) wide. Fill with a sphagnum moss, packing tightly since the tube needs to be quite solid. Wrap the netting around the moss and twist the cut wire ends around the netting to secure.

▲ BACKING FOAM BLOCK: Place moss and wire covered block face down. Cut a piece of double thickness black plastic a little larger than the block. Place over the base of the block and pin to the sides with wire pins made from 18 gauge wires cut into short lengths and bent in half. The plastic should not overlap the base onto the sides by more than 1.2cm ($^{1}/_{2}$in). The backing protects any surface upon which the block may be placed.

▲ ATTACHING BOWS: If you decide you wish to attach
fabric bows to baskets you can make a harder bow by
dipping it in Polyvinyl acetate (PVA) which can be bought
in most craft shops.

▲ CUTTING STEMS: To cut Eucalyptus, hold the leaves back and cut as close as possible to the next set of leaves. Repeat all the way down the stem until the latter begins to thicken. This procedure allows the maximum use of the stem. With multi-branched stems, cut undivided heads for use as they are, or small sprigs with 5cm (2in) stems to be wired for use in head-dresses. Stems 12.5-15cm (5-6in) in length are suitable for standard arrangements.

▶ BAY LEAF BALL: Select several medium-sized fresh bay leaves and a medium-sized dry foam ball. Glue leaves to the ball using transparent-drying adhesive, beginning in the middle, generously overlapping the leaves. Slot other leaves behind and cover the ball completely. The leaves will shrink when they dry, so it is important to overlap them sufficiently.

▶ WIRING A POT: Place a small piece of dry foam into a terracotta pot so that it fits snugly. Thread an 18 gauge wire through the bottom of the pot and between the foam and the side of the pot. The pot can then be wired onto a basket, moss rope or wreath.

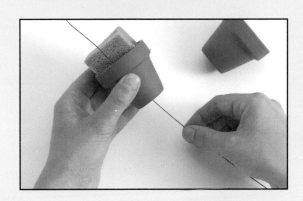

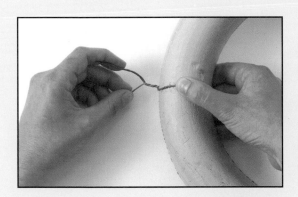

◀ WREATH WIRING: Cover an 18 gauge wire with stem binding tape and wrap around a wreath once only. Twist the ends of the wire tightly, so that the wire cannot move around the ring. Leave the ends of the wire apart so that they can be twisted onto a hook, around a curtain rail or whatever the wreath will be hung from. If the wreath is very thick and one wire is not enough, twist two wires together and cover with stem binding tape.

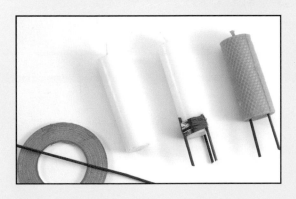

◀ MOUNTING CANDLES: If using chunky beeswax candles, simply insert two or three pieces of cane into the bottom of the candle by not more than 2.5cm (1in). Attach legs to other thick candles by cutting 10cm (4in) pieces of cane. Hold one piece against the side of the candle and bind onto the candle with green adhesive tape. Then add the next 'leg' and bind as before. When all legs are in place, bind all together a few more times to secure. Legs can be attached to narrow candles, but candle holders are more practical.

Wiring

When decorating with or arranging dried flowers, it is best to attach the flowers, seedheads etc – either singly or in bunches – to lengths of wire. Wiring also helps to create a more solid arrangement, as opposed to an airy, wispy effect. You will need 18 or 22 gauge stem wires, the 18 gauge being the strongest.

Take a bunch of dried material and cut stems to the required length – usually 12.5-17.5cm (5-7in). Hold stems together tightly at the bottom between thumb and forefinger. Bend a wire about two-thirds of the way along its length to form a loop. Place the loop under the bunch and hold in place with the third finger. Firmly twist the longer portion of the wire 5 or 6 times around the bunch, but not too tightly as to break the stems. Cinnamon sticks are available in a variety of sizes. Roll a bunch together in the hand to make them fit together. Hold the bunch tightly, and bind with wire.

When making head-dresses and small garlands use silver wires since they are fine, but firm enough to take the weight of small flowers. Silver wire comes in two thicknesses – the thicker is best. Cut flowers from stems, either singly or in bunches. Hold firmly between thumb and forefinger. Make a loop in a length of wire and hold under the short stem. Wind one end around the length of stem about six times keeping the wire taut.

To make a circlet overlap two wires by at least 10cm (4in). Twist a silver wire around the thicker wire, beginning at the top. Bind the entire length with stem binding tape. Bend one end of the wire into a loop and the other end into a hook.

To wire a walnut, dip the end of a 22 gauge wire into latex-based adhesive, then push into the nut base where the two halves join. Leave to dry. Small and medium-sized cones are wired with 22 gauge wires; larger cones require 18 gauge wires. Trim the stems of artichokes to 2.5cm (1in) in length. Wind the wire through the leaves at the base of cones and artichokes and twist the ends around the stem. Single flowers, such as roses, are wired in the same way as bunches.

Tightly wind stem binding tape twice around the top of a wired stem or bunch to cover the wire. Hold firmly between thumb and forefinger and with the other hand, pull the tape downwards so that it stretches. Turn the stem between thumb and forefinger while continuing to pull the tape downwards so that it twists around the length of wire.

1 Fill a pot three-quarters full with nylon-reinforced plaster. Set the main trunk in the centre of the pot, then branches around the trunk. Wire the branches to the trunk at the bottom and top. Cut a hole the same circumference as the trunk and approximately 5cm (2in) deep in a dry foam ball. Cut a piece of wire netting large enough to cover the ball. Wrap around the ball keeping the hole clear of wire.

2 Squeeze some glue from a glue gun into the hole and push the ball onto the trunk. Leave to dry. Thread a 22 gauge wire through the netting at the ball base and around the trunk. Twist the ends to secure. Repeat at equal intervals around the trunk.

3 Push wired items or stems into the ball beginning at the middle top. Work around and down, keeping the dried materials very close together.

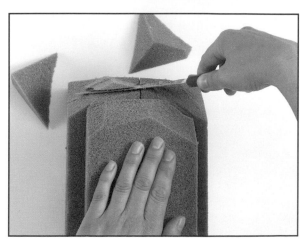

4 To create an unusual topiary, select dry foam blocks to give the required size. Glue blocks together using a glue gun. When dry, cut the foam to a desired shape. A slightly oval shape is effective for a moss topiary. Treat in the same way as the foam ball.

▲ MAKING A POSY HANDLE: To make a bridesmaid's posy handle: Leave a free length of ribbon 25cm (10in) in length, hold ribbon to the top of the handle and run the remainder of the ribbon downwards over the bottom of the handle, then upwards to the top of the handle. Hold both parts of the ribbon together with one hand. With the other hand, wrap the uncut ribbon down the handle. At this stage, the ribbon should be wrong side facing. At the bottom of the handle, fold over the excess ribbon and wrap with the ribbon which should be twisted so that the right side is now facing. Work upwards to the handle top and tie the ribbon onto the free length. Make a simple bow and tie to the top of the handle with a double knot. Insert a long pearl-ended pin into the centre of the bow and push up through the posy.

Spring and Summer

The summer seasons offer a profusion of beautiful blooms for drying and combining to create stunning arrangements. Empty fireplaces can be made into special focal points and plain walls decorated with a posy of pickings. Spring also heralds Easter – a perfect time for a special flower arrangement.

You will need:
A rectangular piece of wood or standard sized tray
Sphagnum moss, fresh Bung and lychin moss
Artificial mushrooms
1 stem artificial berries

▲ A country bunny decoration makes an appropriate centrepiece for Easter. If you intend to move him around glue the bung and lychin moss to the sphagnum moss.

Lay a thick layer of moss over the tray or board and bind in place with black reel wire. Complete one side then turn over and cover the other.

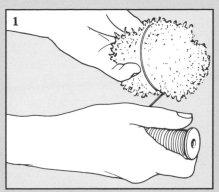

1 To make the bunny tightly bind a handful of moss. add more moss and bind until the body is complete. Make ears and tail in the same way and bind onto body. Use berries for eyes and nose.

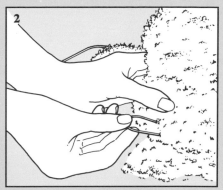

2 Cut several 18 gauge wires into three pieces and bend each into a hairpin shape. Use to pin the bunny to the tray.

▲ Present a gift of fresh or potted herbs or other plants in a woodland inspired box. Select a sturdy fruit or moss box and bind sphagnum moss to the sides with black reel wire. Line box with thick plastic or a plant tray.

You will need:
3 bunches glycerined Eucalyptus
3 bunches cat mint
80 peach roses
15 pomegranates
Sphagnum moss
3 candles
2 m (2¹/₄ yd) white muslin

◄ Wire flowers and foliage in bunches with 22 gauge wires and cover with stem binding tape. Wire pomegranates with 18 gauge wires.

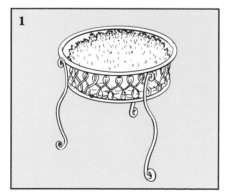

1 Place muslin inside container and drape heavily around sides but keep flat on bottom. Place foam on top and cover with sphagnum moss.

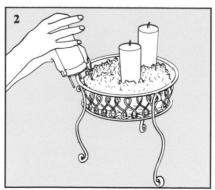

2 Cut green canes into 10cm (4in) pieces. Tape cane pieces to bottom of candles (page 19). Group candles centrally.

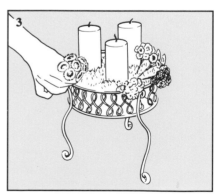

3 Position dried material leaving at least 7.5cm (3in) of candle visible.

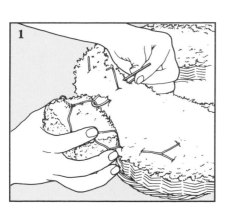

You will need:
6 mini terracotta pots
2 bunches Alchemilla
1 bunch blue larkspur
40 yellow roses
12 dark purple peonies
10 pomegranates
Large bag cinnamon sticks
Sphagnum moss
1 m (1¹/₈ yd) narrow rope
1 m (1¹/₈ yd) blue silk

▲ Wire roses, larkspur and Alchemilla in small bunches; wire cinnamon sticks in pairs and pomegranates. Trim stems of peonies – there is no need to wire them.

1 Make a 7.5cm (3in) moss rope (page 14). Wire to rim of basket. Cut a foam block into eighths. Cover pieces in moss and wire netting (Page 16). Wire at intervals to rope. Fill pots with foam and wire up (Page 19). Attach to moss rope close to blocks.

2 Drape fabric between blocks and secure in place with 22 gauge wires. Fill blocks and pots with dried material. Twist the decorative rope at intervals around the fabric swags.

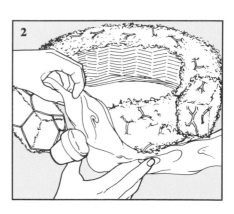

▲ This attractive ring brings the suggestion of a fresh spring morning.

You will need:
A dry foam ring
Bung moss
Button chrysanthemums

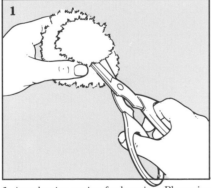

1 Attach wire to ring for hanging. Place ring on a well-protected surface. Trim root base from moss.

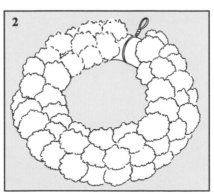

2 Squeeze a small amount of glue onto underside of moss. Position clumps close together on ring – hold in position until set.

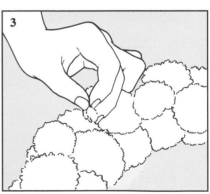

3 Leave 2.5cm (1in) of bare ring for a ribbon bow (pages 16-17). Glue on button chrysanthemums in between the moss clumps.

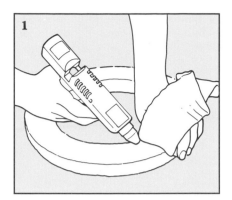

1 Cover underside of ring in fabric. Glue to sides of ring to a level of 1cm ($^{1}/_{2}$in). Apply glue to the reverse of the fabric and press in place. Be careful not to burn your fingers.

2 Wire flowers, tree mushrooms and artificial mushrooms and cover with stem binding tape. Trim wires so that they do not pierce underside of wreath when mounted. Then carefully mount each wire.

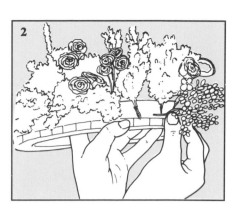

◀ This pair of elegant rose topiaries would make an unusual mantelpiece display for a social gathering.

You will need:
2 birch poles 2.5-3.75cm (1-1^1/2in) in diameter, 30cm (12in) in length
2 10cm (4in) foam balls
200 roses on stems
A little moss
1 m (1^1/8 yd) ribbon

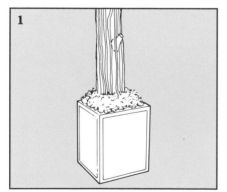

1 Line two pots with plastic and fill a half to three-quarters full with nylon-reinforced plaster (page 22). Cut roses from stems leaving 2.5cm (1in) of stem on flowers. Trim leaves from stems. Push pole into plaster. Push stems into plaster and wire to pole.

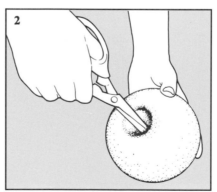

2 Cut a small hole in foam ball, fill with glue and push onto pole. Leave to set.

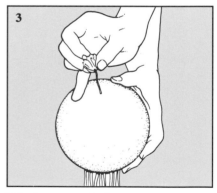

3 Push roses into ball starting at the top. Tie ribbon around poles and cover plaster with moss.

▲ These are romantic gifts or decorations with a distinctively Victorian feel. Make a bow (page 16) and push wire stems into the bottom of the ball. Wire a loop of fabric and insert into the ball top to hang. A plain wooden picture frame can be enhanced by gluing on lychin moss and rose heads.

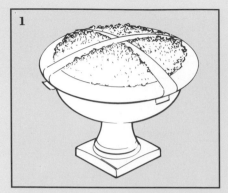

1 Push a slightly over-sized block of foam into pot. Trim corners, cover lightly with moss and tape in place.

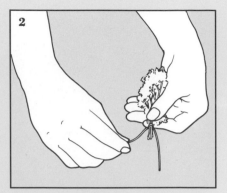

2 Wire flowers in small bunches with 22 gauge wires to make 7.5cm (3in) stems and bind with stem binding tape. There is no need to wire peonies.

3 Cut fruit from stem, wire and bind as Step 2. Start with peonies then gradually add the other flowers.

You will need:
2 bunches blue larkspur
1 bunch chamomile daisy
20 assorted roses
5 pink peonies
5 dark purple peonies
1 stem artificial fruits

▲ A subtle but beautiful miniature arrangement. Bend the bunches at the front forwards over the edge of the pot to create a softer effect. When arranging, stand back from the arrangement at intervals to check the overall shape.

▲ These miniature terracotta pot arrangements would make unusual table decorations for a celebration of romance. Fill the pots tightly with foam and insert trimmed rose stems, small bunches of marjoram or lavender. Push a short length of green cane into the bottom of the candle and insert into the foam.

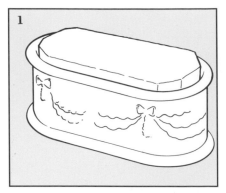

1 Cut a dry foam block in half, trim and push into container; make sure it fits tightly. Cover with moss and tape in place.

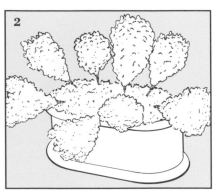

2 Position 8 bunches – 2-3 in the centre and the remainder around edge – to create the arrangement's basic shape.

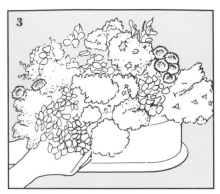

3 Intersperse hydrangea heads making them slightly shorter than the other bunches. Add remainder of flowers.

You will need:
2 bunches Ambrosinia
2 bunches scabious
20 stems large headed roses
8 stems yellow kangaroo paws
4 heads hydrangea

▲ Dimension is added to this arrangement using the trick of lowering the height of the hydrangea heads in relation to the other flowers.

You will need:
3 branches 2.5cm (1in) in
diameter, 25cm (10in) in length
8 bunches glycerined
Eucalyptus
A little bung or lychin moss

▲ An unusual foliage topiary. Eucalyptus is attractive both for
its silver blue-green colour and its interesting leaf formation.

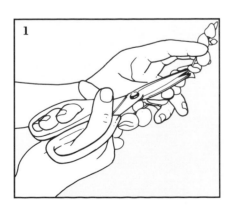

1 Cut the stems of Eucalyptus into short
lengths taking care to cut the stems as close
as possible to the next set of leaves. This
enables the whole stem to be used.

2 Wire bunches of 3 Eucalyptus pieces
tightly together with 22 gauge wire. Cut off
excess wire to leave a clear 5cm (2 in) of
stem. Make the topiary base (page 22) with
the branches and either a foam ball or oval
shape. Push the Eucalyptus bunches into
the foam as close together as possible.
Cover the quick-drying plaster with moss.

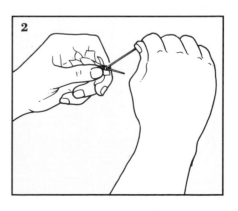

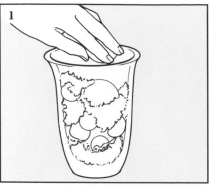

1 Place bung moss into a vase then some pebbles to fill one-third. Add a block of dry foam. Add more moss and pebbles.

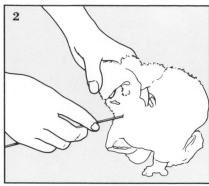

2 Wire cinnamon sticks and other drieds (pages 20-21). Bind with stem binding tape. Make holes in sea sponges for wiring.

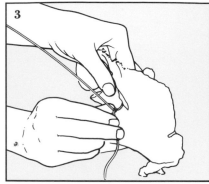

3 Push wire through the holes and twist. Position sea sponge, then other material. Add soaked and squeezed moss.

You will need:
2 bunches globe amaranth
18 stems Anaphalis (pearl everlasting)
15 stems cones
10 cinnamon sticks
9 proteas
6 artichoke heads
3 large sea sponges
Ground lychin and bung moss
Pebbles

► The lychin moss should be soaked in warm water and squeezed as dry as possible before being used in the arrangement. It will dry in place, so there is no need to wire.

You will need:
3 bunches artificial berries
2 bunches lavender
1 bunch Achillea
1 bunch marjoram
30 stems peach roses
3 heads hydrangea

▲ A pastel-shaded arrangement for a side or occasional table. Fill a glass container with sphagnum moss, then place a piece of foam on top and tape in place. Now add the flowers and artificial berries.

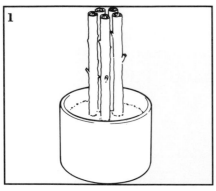

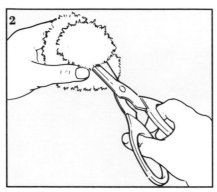

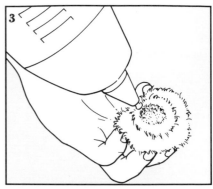

1 Make a topiary base (page 22) – the branches should extend 20cm (8in) above pot rim. Attach foam ball.

2 Trim off the root part of the bung moss clumps, so they are easier to handle.

3 Squeeze glue from a glue gun onto underside of moss. Place clumps onto foam as close together as possible. Keep fingers away from hot glue. Cover the quick drying plaster with moss.

You will need:
3-6 narrow branches or twig
approx 27.5cm (11in) in leng
Bung moss
A little lychin or sphagnum m

◀ Most topiaries can be ma
in a variety of sizes and shape
Foam blocks can be cut into
different shapes and glued
together to form a rounded
oblong shape instead of using
foam ball.

▲ These dazzling topiaries will bring summer cheer to the home at any time of year. Hair spray will prevent these rather delicate flowers from dropping.

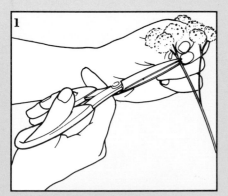

1 Make 2 topiary bases (page 22). Attach a half foam block to each pole. Take one stem of Santolina at a time and trim off heads leaving 2.5cm (1in) of stem.

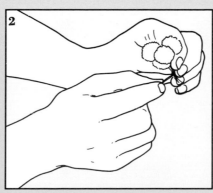

2 Carefully wire the heads into bunches of 3-4 (pages 20-21).

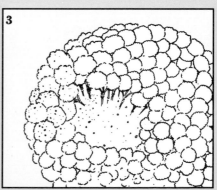

3 Insert bunches into foam as close together as possible. Cover plaster with moss, then spray flowers with hair spray.

1 Push foam into container to fit tightly leaving 10cm (4in) visible above pot rim. Cover with moss.

2 Create the basic shape with some of the taller items at back and shorter flowers around edge.

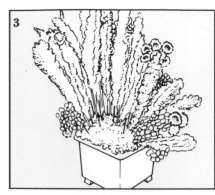

3 To judge the required length of an item on a green cane, measure it against pot before trimming. Position remaining flowers.

You will need:
4 bunches cream zinnias
4 bunches Ambrosinia
4 bunches assorted roses
3 bunches globe thistles
2 bunches sunflowers
14 small heads hydrangea

▲ This is a facing, flat-backed arrangement to be viewed from the front and sides only. It is therefore an ideal arrangement to fill the gaping hole of a fireplace during the summer months.

▲ Sunflowers have so much drama, why not preserve their
beauty to admire throughout the year. Fill a terracotta pot
with foam, cover with moss and pin in place. Trim sunflower
stems to the required length and create a basic framework
for the arrangement with a couple of stems at the centre
back and a couple either side. Then fill in between with
other stems. Do not strip the stems of leaves – their shapes
break up the solidity of the arrangement.

Autumn and Winter

Enhance your home during the autumn and winter months with rich arrangements. Choose warm tones and mellow shades to make the most of the seasons. Table decorations and topiaries feature fiery red chilli peppers, and plump artificial fruits.

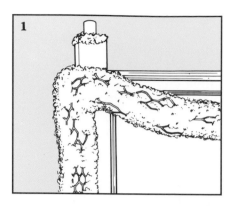

1 Make a moss rope to form the swag, and secure in place with nails threading wire through the back of the fireplace. Twist fabric loosely around the rope and wire in place at the ends of the tube.

2 Mount nuts onto wire stems and wire together in large bunches. Fill small terracotta pots with walnuts and roses. Wire fruits in bunches and cinamon sticks, and add these to the rope with wire.

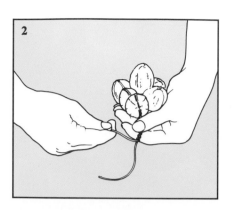

▲ This dramatic winter fireplace scene is completed with the addition of cinnamon bundles so that it covers the wire which attaches the ribbon to the shelf.

▶ This arrangement is perfect for a dull corner during the winter months. The rich colours of the fruit combine dramatically with the deep red roses. Remember not to leave the arrangement unattended when the candles are lit.

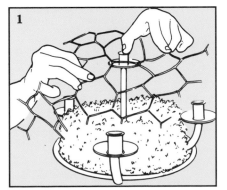

1 Place the foam blocks on top and bottom levels of candelabra and cover lightly with moss. Cut a circular piece of wire netting and place over the foam on the top level. Cut a second circle of wire netting and fit around the centre stem of the candelabra to cover foam. Wire netting to shelf edges.

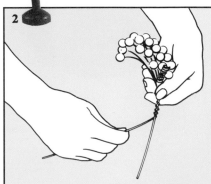

2 Wire roses into groups of three, chillies into groups of three to nine and bunches of grapes singly. Position the grapes first then fruits, roses and finally the chillies.

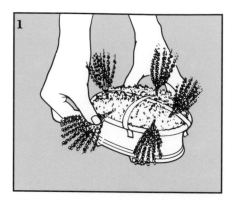

1 Place small pieces of foam into container, cover with moss and tape in place. Wire small bunches of Queen Anne's lace, lavender, roses, clover and Delphinium with 22 gauge wires. Cut each hydrangea head into 5 pieces. Wire each with 22 gauge wire. Bind all stems with stem binding tape. Position about 6 lavender bunches to create basic shape.

2 Fill in with remainder of flowers pushing them deeper into foam, if necessary, to make shorter than lavender.

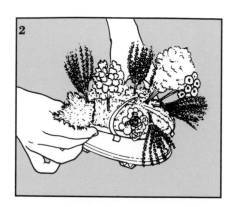

▲ A charming, compact arrangement suitable for a bedside table. The lavender heads should break out slightly from the otherwise smooth outline.

You will need:
2 bunches Queen Anne's lace or
cow parsley
1 bunch lavender
1 bunch purple clover
30 assorted rose
2 heads artificial hydrangea
1 stem blue Delphinium

▲ A dainty and delightful basket arrangement that would make an elegant addition to a treasured friend or relative's bedside or dressing table.

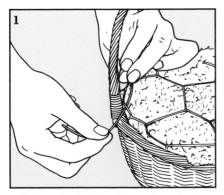

1 Cut block of oasis to fit snugly in basket. Cover lightly with moss and wire netting.

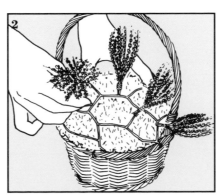

2 Position bunches of either lavender or marjoram to create the basic shape.

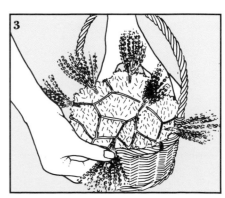

3 At the front of the basket, gently bend the bunches downwards to cover the edge. Then infill with remaining flowers.

You will need:
40 assorted hydrangea heads –
60-70 heads for an all-round
arrangement
Bung moss

◀ This arrangement is most
effective when different
varieties and colours of
hydrangea are used in
combination.

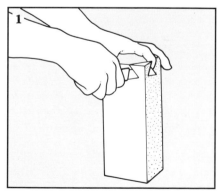

1 Push foam blocks into urn to fill. The
middle block should be approximately 5cm
(2in) higher than others. Cut off top corners
using a craft knife.

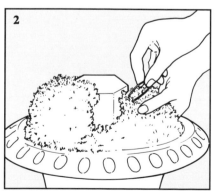

2 Cover foam lightly with bung moss and
pin in place. Wire all except 3-4 hydrangea
heads onto green canes; wire remainder
with 18 gauge wires. Bind with brown stem
binding tape.

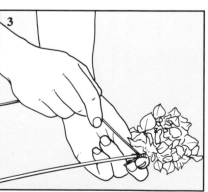

3 Place first hydrangea in centre, then a
few each side. Fill in with rest of canes.
Add wired heads around edge and bend
over urn rim.

▲ To make this spectacular lavender urn, place a block of
foam into the container making sure that at least half of the
block is above the pot rim. Round off corners. Divide each
lavender bunch into 4 and trim steps to 10-12.5cm (4-5in)
in length. Wire with 22 gauge wires and bind with stem
binding tape (pages 20-21). Place the first bunches at the
top of the foam and work downwards keeping the bunches
tightly packed.

▲ Use a piece of silk or satin to line a wire basket. Trim the excess fabric around the rim and using a glue gun, glue the fabric to the rim. Glue the ribbon around the rim to cover, making loops in the ribbon as you work. If the basket is oval, make sure that the ribbon ends meet at one flatter side of the basket. Glue on flowerheads in a group, and a matching group on the opposite side of the basket. Additionally, you could make roses from scraps of the lining fabric by folding and gluing to hold. Intersperse fabric roses in amongst the dried flowerheads.

You will need:
9 assorted roses
6 zinnias
3 m (3^1/$_3$ yd) ribbon
Fabric to line basket

You will need:
2 bunches open cones
1 bunch dry Eucalyptus
1 bunch small cones
3 stems artificial poly-dried peonies
3 stems artificial poly-dried roses
3 stems artificial fruits
3 stems artificial grapes
$^1/_2$ m ($^1/_2$ yd) red velvet
$^1/_2$ m ($^1/_2$ yd) red paper ribbon

◀ Aim for a fairly solid, high-domed shape when positioning the flowers. Then intersperse the fruits and cones, and lastly the Eucalyptus to lighten the arrangement.

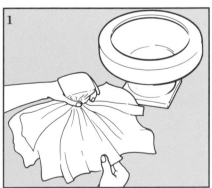

1 Wrap footed bowl in velvet, wire around neck of bowl and cover with ribbon.

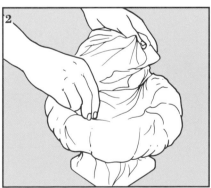

2 Turn pot upright and tuck excess fabric into top of pot.

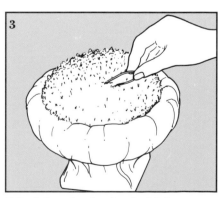

3 Push foam into bowl to fit tightly, cover with moss and pin in place. Wire cones and fruit of one stem (pages 20-21). Other material can remain on original stems.

You will need:
2 bunches woodland cones
1 bunch green marjoram
1 bunch marjoram
20 stems red species roses
20 stems yellow roses
6 narrow beeswax candles

▲ Bring a warm glow to your winter table with this small beeswax candle arrangements. Fill the container with foam, cover with moss and pin or tape in place. Insert pieces of green cane into the bottom of the candles (page 19) and group in the centre of the foam. Wire dried items in bunches (pages 20-21), and group to make a 'collar' around the candles, bending the lower bunches well down over the container's edge.

▲ A posy with a difference – the stems are twisted so that they splay, enabling it to stand upright. This arrangement makes a dramatic centrepiece for a larger-scale celebration dining or buffet table. Before you begin, separate stems of dried material so they can be picked up easily with one hand. Hold a small bunch of stems in one hand, then add one stem at a time, spiralling the stems as you go. Flowers should get shorter around outer edge. Bind stems together with wire or stem binding tape. Cover with ribbon and a bow. Then trim stems so posy can stand.

▲ A winter extravaganza! Pack the bunches of dried
flowers close together to achieve a solid arrangement with a
smooth outline overall.

1 Wire about 80% of ingredients in groups
onto green canes. Cut fruit from stems and
wire onto green canes in groups of 3. Wire
the remaining material in groups with 18
gauge stem wire. Cover all wires with stem
binding tape.

2 Using five of the green canes, create
basic shape, ie first bunch in centre top, the
other four between centre and sides.
Position the wired bunches around the edge
of container. Bend forwards slightly to soften
hard edge of pot. Fill in framework with
remainder of material on canes.

▲ In this opulent arrangement, bunches of crimson, deep pink, pale pink and pale yellow roses are packed closely together to form a solid domed shape, broken at intervals with contrasting sprigs of blue-green Eucalyptus.

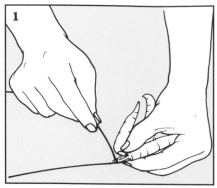

1 Using silver reel wire, wire bunches of chillies together, then wire with stem wires and bind. Wire a bunch of marjoram to ring.

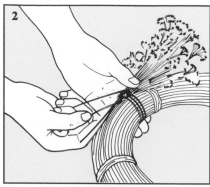

2 Trim stems of marjoram and rosemary to 17.5cm (7in) in length; bay leaves can be shorter. Attach a wire to hang the wreath.

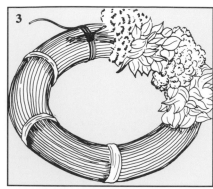

3 Add chillies, bay then rosemary. Repeat pattern until wreath is complete.

▲ This inviting herbal wreath makes the ideal gift for any cook. It will bring natural fragrance to the kitchen as well as a ready supply of herbs for culinary purposes.

▲ Wire-edged ribbon is excellent for dried flower
arranging in that it can be creatively shaped.

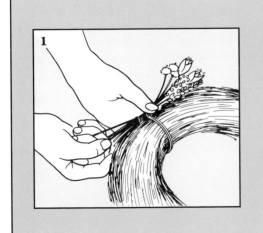

1 Bind an 18 gauge wire with tape and
attach to ring for hanging. Wire woodland
drieds into bunches of three and bind. Cut
Eucalyptus into 10-12.5cm (4-5 in) long
pieces. Cut proteas from stems leaving
7.5cm (3in) of stem. Tie a length of green
garden twine to ring for binding on stems.

2 Place a few stems of Eucalyptus onto ring
and bind tightly with twine. Add a couple of
proteas, then add a woodland bunch. Bind
tightly once more. Continue until ring is
covered. Make nine small double-looped
bows (Page 16) and one large bow for the
top. Insert bows into wreath at intervals.

► A commonplace frame for a special photograph can be enhanced by gluing on dried tree lychins. They echo the yellowing tonal qualities of an ageing photograph.

1 To make mirror frame: Drape fabric around mirror frame and glue in place once a good shape has been achieved.

2 Cut bases of some of magnolia leaves, apply glue and insert into fabric folds. Group other magnolia leaves and glue onto fabric at intervals. Cut sunflowers from stems as close as possible to the heads. Place at intervals around the frame, some in groups, and glue in place when satisfied with arrangement. Add a few sunflower leaves to lighten the effect.

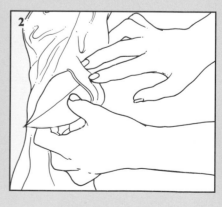

You can transform any plain wooden-framed mirror in this way. Adapt the colour scheme to co-ordinate with your interior decor by using alternative flowers and fabric.

You will need:
1 wooden-framed mirror
40-50 red-dyed magnolia leaves
36 sunflowers
3 m (3$^1/_3$ yd) fabric

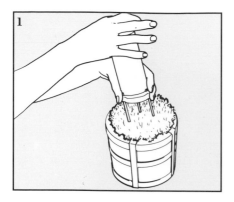

1 Cut foam block in half and push into pot. Trim corners if too big. Cover lightly in moss and pin in place. Cut a green cane into 3 pieces and tape to bottom of candle. Place centrally.

2 Cut artificial fruits off stems retaining wire stem. Wire large singly; small in groups of 3 or 5. Place artichokes, fruits then roses.

You will need:
6 stems small assorted artificial fruits
5 artichokes
3 stems large assorted artificial fruits
3 open poly-dried roses
1 candle

▲ If the artificial fruit stem is hand wrapped, it is best to unravel the wrapping. In this case you will have long enough wires on the undivided fruits not to have to wire them up.

▲ Turn an ordinary wicker basket into an original and highly attractive gift by decorating the outside with a colourful variety of dried and artificial items. For this design, we used tree mushrooms, white paper flowers, tree lychin moss, small poppy seedheads, florets of artificial hydrangea and petals of a 'Minuet' rose. Simply apply glue from a glue gun to the bottom of each item and position on the basket.

Everyday Arrangements

Even when there is no special occasion to celebrate it is nice to be able to decorate the home with stunning but simple flower arrangements, to make the house into a home. Dried flowers offer the opportunity to create a wide variety of displays which will last forever.

▲ Decorate a brightly coloured box with a matching ribbon and fill with a fragarant and eye-catching pot pourri mixture, perhaps consisting of flowers and herbs gathered from your garden throughout the spring and summer.

▶ This magnificent wall plaque makes an original interior decoration. It could be hung horozontally in a suitable location for extra drama.

You will need:
2 bunches dried grasses
2 bunches morrison
2 bunches glycerined Eucalyptus
1 bunch red species roses
26-30 glycerined magnolia leaves
9 proteas
4 sunflowers
1 string chillies

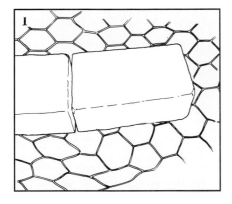

1 To make the plaque base, cut foam blocks in half to form 2 shallow pieces. Cut a strip of wire netting slightly longer than 3-4 foam blocks end to end and wide enough to wrap around the width of one block.

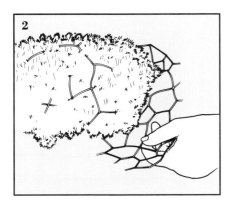

2 Lay wire netting flat and cover lightly with moss. Place blocks onto moss end to end. Bring sides of netting in to meet middle top of foam. Twist cut ends of wire together. Make sure netting is tight around foam; if not tighten at this stage. Cover underside of plaque with plastic and attach a hanging wire covered with stem binding tape.

You will need:
A branch 7.5cm (3in) in diameter, 45cm
(18 in) in length
Thin branches of contorted willow
A large quantity of glycerined magnolia
leaves
Bung moss
1m (1¹/₈yd) fabric

▶ A spectacular topiary destined to be the
focal point of any interior. Choose a
luxurious fabric in a rich colour for
wrapping the base.

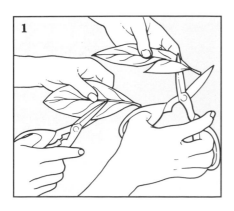

1 Magnolia leaves come in several different
sizes. Choose medium-sized leaves. Cut
larger leaves to size by trimming the side of
the leaf leaving enough stem to wire.

2 Hold leaves in groups of three, splayed
slightly at the top. Wire together using 22
gauge wires. Push into foam ball starting at
the top. The right sides of leaves should face
inwards. Keep turning topiary while adding
bunches of leaves. When complete, wrap pot
in fabric. Cover inside of pot with moss.

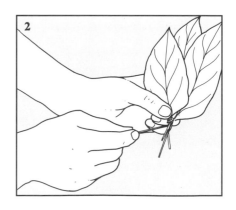

▲ You will need approximately 50 hydrangea heads to
make this large-scale topiary. Follow the instructions on
page 22 to make the topiary base. Insert the trimmed stems
of the hydrangea heads into the foam to cover. Cover the
plaster in the container with bung moss.

You will need:
2 bunches green marjoram
2 bunches glycerined Eucalyptus
2 bunches Agastache mexicana
2 bunches dahlias
40 stems dark pink roses
8 stems artificial fruits
4 heads hydrangea
Hydrangea florets

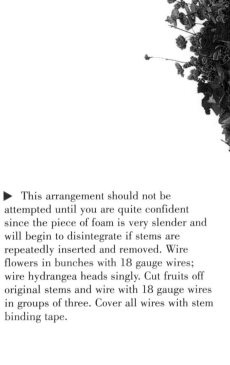

▶ This arrangement should not be attempted until you are quite confident since the piece of foam is very slender and will begin to disintegrate if stems are repeatedly inserted and removed. Wire flowers in bunches with 18 gauge wires; wire hydrangea heads singly. Cut fruits off original stems and wire with 18 gauge wires in groups of three. Cover all wires with stem binding tape.

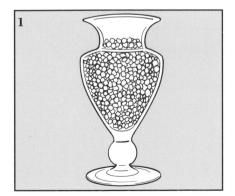

1 Fill vase up with hydrangea florets.

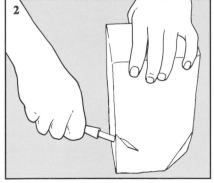

2 Cut approximately three-quarters of a foam block in half lengthways. Cut off bottom corners.

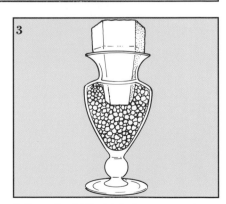

3 Foam should fit tightly into vase neck leaving 7.5cm (3in) above rim. Fill to rim with florets pushing down sides of foam with round-edged knife.

▶ For an unusual decoration around the home, why not make an elegant moss topiary tree which can be decorated with miniature beads. Follow the instructions on pages 22-23 to make the topiary base, but use a foam cone in place of the ball. Glue beads onto the moss to complete. You could make two matching trees to stand either side of a fireplace.

You will need:
2 bunches marjoram
2 bunches Ageratum
1 bunch green golden rod
1 bunch Achillea
20 roses
7 peonies
3 heads hydrangea
1m (1¹/₈yd) x 30cm (12in) wide silk

◀ A bouquet of sumptuous summer pickings which can be hung on a wall or door for all to admire.

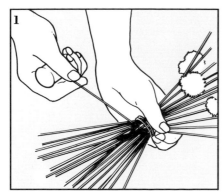

1 Gather up a few stems at a time in one hand and wire together just below hand. Continue adding stems, reducing length of extending stems. Secure with wire.

2 Make a bow from silk (pages 16-17) and wire to front of bunch.

3 Add wired stems and bunches above bow to give fullness, bending forward slightly.

▲ A Caribbean cocktail of flowers dramatically set off by
the deep blue fabric. Line the basket with the latter, laying
it flat on the bottom, but draping around the sides. Then add
foam and cover with moss. Create your basic shape with
wired bunches of blue larkspur.

You will need:
3 bunches blue larkspur
2 bunches yellow button chrysanthemums
1 bunch Celosia
1 bunch Carthamus
40 stems red roses ('Jaguar')
7 pink peonies
7 zinnias
2 heads hydrangea

▲ Napkins can be effectively decorated for a celebration
table using wire-edged ribbon, which can be arranged to
create attractive shapes, flowerheads, cones or seedheads.
Choose colours and textures to coordinate with the overall
colour scheme or theme of the table.

You will need:
5 bunches cones
4 bunches peach roses
3-5 bunches marjoram
3 bunches assorted roses
2 bunches mixed species roses
2 bunches green golden rod
15 cinnamon sticks
7 heads hydrangea
5 stems artificial fruits
1 m (1⅛ yd) silk

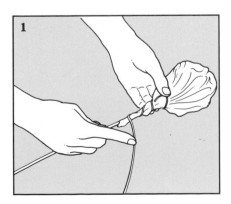

1 Fill pot with foam. Cover with moss and tape in place. Cut the silk into nine squares. Gather up corners, hold tightly together and bind with silver wire. Wire each gathered fabric piece onto a cane using 22 gauge wire. Tuck in rough edges. Bind with binding tape. Wire bunches of flowers, fruits, cones and cinnamon sticks onto canes and bind.

2 Begin at back of pot and place first bunch of flowers three-quarters of the way back from front of pot. Place bunches around edge and middle of arrangement to make a basic framework. Fill in with other canes pushing some in deeper to give dimension.

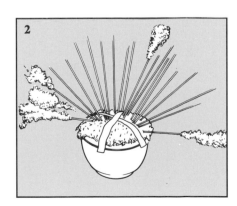

▲ This arrangement is truly red hot! Wire the peppercorns, Ageratum, roses and marigolds in bunches. Wire cones and chillies singly. The latter usually have short stems on which to attach the wire. Make sure that the chillies extend beyond the other elements to create an interesting, spiky outline.

You will need:
7 bunches red marigolds
2 bunches red peppercorns
1 bunch cones
1 bunch Ageratum
1 bunch roses ('Minuet')
20 chillies

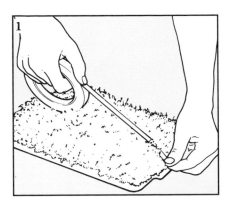

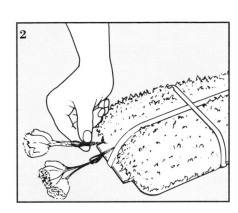

1 Cut a block of foam in half to create a shallow full-width piece. Place on a black plastic tray and cover lightly with moss. Tape moss and foam to tray.

2 Insert flowers into sides of foam at either end of base. Add berries – 2 at each end, one shorter than the other, 2 along each side and 3 on top of the foam. Fill in with remaining material.

▲ Aim for a long, low shape in this arrangement. It would make an excellent centrepiece for a refectory or trestle table – perhaps for a meal or just as a table-top display.

▲ This charming little basket is ideal for a table-top centrepiece or as an unusual fruit bowl. The flowers are simply glued to the rim of the basket. It can be filled with small flowerheads and leaves, or with exotic fruit when they are in season!

You will need:
1 bunch Helichrysum
$^1/_2$ bunch Carthamus
$^1/_2$ bunch cluster-flowered Helichrysum
6 proteas
5 open roses ('Golden Times')
1 stem bright blue Delphinium

You will need:
A piece of plywood approximately
60 x 45cm (2 x 1^1/$_2$ ft)
Assorted dried flowerheads and
artificial fruits
2m (2^2/$_3$yd) heavy green fabric
3m (3^1/$_3$yd) x 3.75cm (1^1/$_2$in) wide
thick cord

◄ This firescreen is easily decorated with a variety of colourful flowerheads and artificial fruits – simply glue them to the fabric. The fabric strip for the piping can be made from short strips of fabric sewn together end to end to form one long strip.

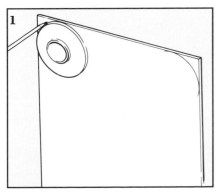

1 Round off corners of wood by drawing around a plate. Cut along the pencil line with a saw.

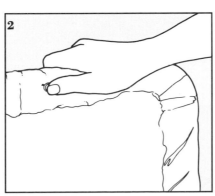

2 Place wood on fabric and trim excess leaving a 5cm (2in) border. Fold border over screen edge and pin or glue.

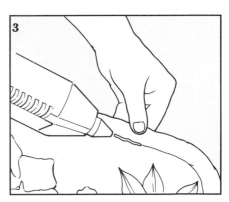

3 Encase cord in a 7.5cm (3in) wide fabric strip the length of screen's perimeter. Glue rough edges of piping to screen back and piping to screen front.

Special Occasions

Dried flowers are a practical and versatile alternative to fresh flowers for a special occasion. The added advantage with dried flowers is that they will avoid the major problem of wilting on a hot summer day, which makes them perfect for garden parties and special head-dresses.

▼ Delight a loved one or a bride with a collection of pretty and fragrant homemade pomanders. Cut a square or circular piece of muslin and fill with lavender or pot pourri. Gather the edges of the muslin together and tie with narrow string. Trim excess muslin if necessary. Place the bag upright in the centre of a piece of fabric. gather up around the edges and fasten at the neck with silver reel wire. Cover with co-ordinating ribbon and tie the end in a loop.

▲ This sumptous heart-shaped basket filled with fragarent pot pourri will make a memorial engagement gift.

You will need:
30-35 roses
2 heads of hydrangea
2m (2 1/4yd) wire edged ribbon

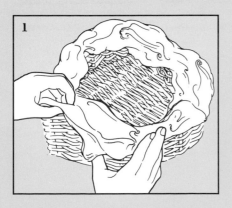

1 Line the basket with a sheet of plastic, then cover with fabric. Glue the ribbon onto the basket.

2 Cut roses from stems entirely. Squeeze a little glue onto the underside of each rose and hold in place on the basket. When dry carefully remove any strands of glue.

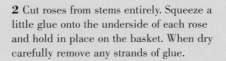
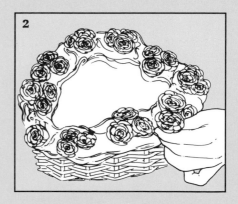

◀ A delightful decoration for a celebratory bottle of bubbly. It is important to select vividly-coloured flowers to contrast with the colour of the bottle. Lay flowers out on your work surface to see how they work together before wiring.

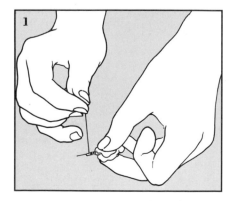

1 Select a few small brightly-coloured flowers and bind with silver wires. Bind with stem binding tape.

2 Bend an 18 gauge wire into a hoop, overlap ends and twist together. Cover with stem binding tape. Bind flowers onto hoop one at a time, making 3 or 4 twists then trimming excess wire. Continue until hoop is full. To add last flower, pull other flowers away slightly, then wire on the flower.

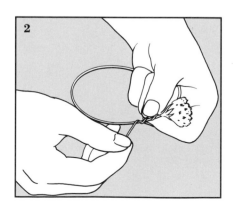

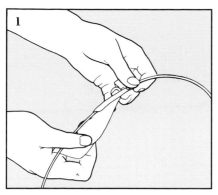

1 Bend an 18 gauge wire into a hoop, overlap ends and twist together. Cover with stem binding tape. Bind hoop with ribbon.

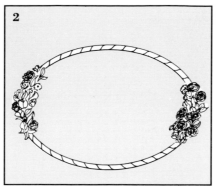

2 Cut flowers from stems at the top and spread on a tray. Measure 10cm (4in) either side of the top middle point of hoop. Begin gluing small flowerheads to hoop.

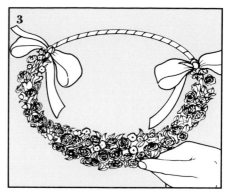

3 Use larger flowers at the centre bottom for balance. Make two small bows and attach to the hoop on either side.

▲ This elegant hoop makes an unusual alternative to the more traditional posy. The bows can be omitted for a simpler, cleaner effect.

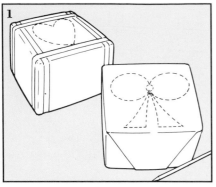

1 Wrap parcels and decorate with ribbon. Draw outlines of the designs in pencil onto the parcels.

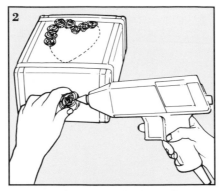

2 Using a glue gun, apply glue to the bottom of each flower and position.

3 Glue on nuts and fruits one at a time.

▲ Gift packages for any occasion can be transformed from the commonplace with the simple addition of dried flowerheads and other material. Keep the glue gun away from the parcel when gluing the flowers and be careful not to burn your fingers when applying hot glue to small dried items. You can use a strong, tube adhesive instead, but avoid any direct contact with the fingers.

▲ Give your gifts a chic personal touch by gluing dried flowers – either single heads or bunches – onto giftwrap or decorative ribbon. Here, we have used 2 peony heads and a small bunch of lavender with pale blue wire-edged ribbon for the white package and a glycerined mauve anemone with gold ribbon for the marbled box.

▲ A stunning heart-shaped wreath to adorn a wall or door
at a wedding, for Valentines Day or at an anniversary
reception. Wire the rose heads singly with silver wires and
cover with stem binding tape. When wiring the flowers to
the wreath, rest the heart on a work surface.

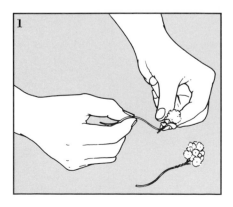

1 Use silver wire to make stems for the
posys of flowers. Use two 18 gauge wires
together and bind with stem binding tape.
Bend wire to form shape. Attach ends by
forming a loop and hook (Page 20)

2 Twist flowers onto heart starting from the
middle top and working outwards and
downwards. Keep the flowers even all the
way around.

For the head-dress you will need:
Tiny bunches of various dried flowers
6-8 thumb sized terracotta pots
Single flowerheads, eg roses, sunflowers and
marigolds
15 x 7.5cm (3inch) squares fabric

▼ Wire tiny bunches and single
flowerheads onto silver wires and cover with
stem binding tape. Wire terracotta pots and
fill each with a wired flowerhead, the wire
end fed through the hole in the pot bottom.
Gather up corners of each fabric square and
wire with silver wire. Bind with stem
binding tape.

▲ When making the posy, once you have wired the stems cover them with stem
binding tape, place flowers in jars – the same type in one jar – to allow
easy access and selection.

1 For the headdress: Make a circlet
(Page 21). Begin at hook end and twist
wired flowers onto circlet. Trim excess wires
as you work. Finish 7.5cm (3in) from loop.

2 For the posy: Wire flowers with 22
gauge wires and cover with stem binding
tape. Take 5-8 stems and tightly bind
together 12.5cm (5in) from the flowerheads
(5-7.5cm/2-3in for small bridesmaids) using
silver reel wire. Whilst turning stems in one
hand, open them out to create a frame. Add
other flowers, binding one stem in place at a
time. Finally, trim wires, bind handle with
tape and ribbon.

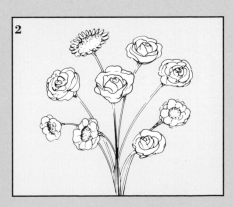

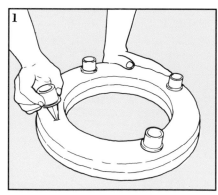

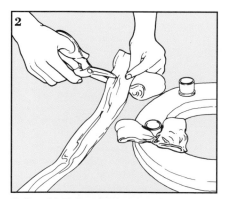

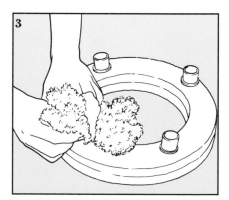

1 Position candleholders at equal distances around ring, pushing bases into foam.

2 Cut ribbon into 8 equal lengths and make single loop bows without tails (page 16). Place 2 bows by each candleholder.

3 Mount candles, then position cones. Add lavender, then marjoram and roses. Complete with plums and gold grapes.

1 Apply a line of glue from a glue gun down the length of corn cobs. Attach at intervals to the wreath.

2 Trim any stem from pomegranates and other fruits as close to fruit as possible. Glue the larger items to wreath. Fill in with small items until wreath is full and chunky. Remember to leave space at top for bow. Make a large double-looped bow and tie onto wreath.

▲ Cover an 18 gauge wire with stem binding tape and twist onto wreath for hanging.

You will need:
A twig wreath 35cm (14in) in diameter
Assorted dried cones
Assorted artificial and dried fruits
Walnuts
3 dried corn cobs
1 m (1 1/8 yd) ribbon

You will need:
7.5-12.5cm (3-5in) dry foam balls
100 roses (for 10cm/4in balls)

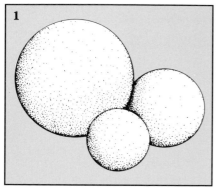

1 Select size of foam ball required. Trim rose stems to 2.5cm (1in) in length.

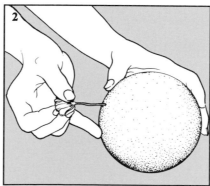

2 Hold ball in palm of the hand. Push roses into foam close together.

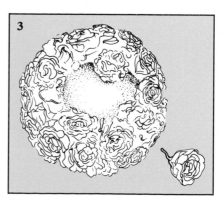

3 Complete one side of ball, turn over and gently continue inserting roses into ball until covered entirely.

▲ Even the smallest size of foam ball requires a great many roses to fully cover it. However, if you wanted to group a few rose balls in a bowl, you could leave the foam bare where it was not visible, to use fewer roses. Drape ribbon or fabric around the balls to conceal any bare patches.

▲ To make a bridesmaid's pomander, wrap a dry-foam ball in a square of fabric, gather at the top and secure with a 22 gauge wire. Trim excess fabric to 10cm (4in) above wire. Fold over and tuck in rough fabric edges. Make a fabric ribbon and tie on. Carefully tuck the flower heads into the wire, then

glue securely. To make a more secure decoration for the pomander, wire flowers onto a wire ring following the instructions for the champagne bottle wreath on page 26, then attach to the pomander around the 'neck'. These dainty decorations are light and easy for junior bridesmaids to hold.

▲ A traditional centrepiece for the festive table. Beeswax candles give off a sweet scent when lit.

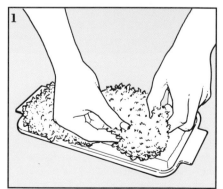

1 Cut block of foam in half to make a shallow, full-width piece. Place on black tray and cover lightly with moss.

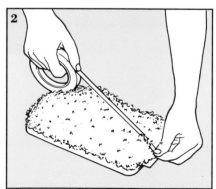

2 Tape foam and moss in place. Cut 2 green canes into 6 pieces. Insert 3 pieces into the bottom of each candle (page 19).

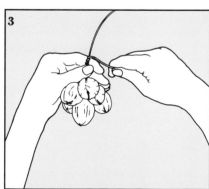

3 Wire cones with 22 gauge wires. Mount walnuts onto wires (page 20) and wire together in groups of 5.

▲ A truly elegant Advent ring. Position candleholders and mount candles. Spray the cones with silver paint and wire. Wire Eucalyptus in bunches and group around the candles. Add cones and fruits. Finally, add the paper flowers to give highlights.

You will need:
30-40 stems poly-dried flowers
3 m (3^1/$_3$ yd) x 3-cm (1^1/$_4$-in) wide ribbon

◄ Wire flowerheads with 22 gauge wires (pages 17-18) – their original stems are far too heavy. Cover wire with stem binding tape and group in jars or vases to make selection easier.

▼ Poly-dried flowers are an effective artificial alternative to real dried flowers. Made from polyester, they are able to withstand considerable wear and tear. Make a head-dress from poly-dried flowers to match the bouquet.

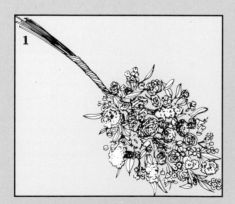

1 Begin with the bottom of the bouquet. Twist wired stems of flowers and leaves onto each other to form a soft, oval-shaped 'tail'. Continue to add stems until the tail is at least 25cm (10in) long. Bend the wire ends downwards to form a handle at least 15cm (6in) away from the flowers.

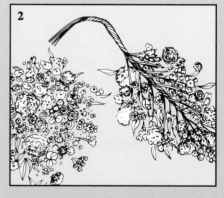

2 Make a light posy 20-25cm (8-10in) in diameter (Page 23) with silver reel wire, bind stem of posy to stem of 'tail' below handle. Hold the bouquet's handle in front of a mirror and add more flowers to fill any gaps. Trim excess wires and cut handle to hand size. Cover well with stem binding tape. Cover with ribbon and add bow.

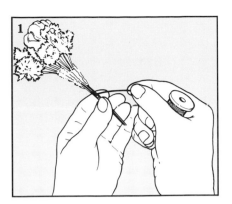

1. Begin with the large rose in the centre and surround with marjoram. Bind the stems together with silver reel wire where your hand is holding the bouquet. Add the next set of flowers and wire again.

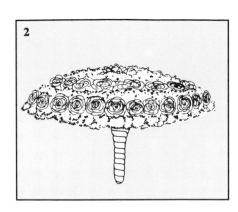

2 Turn the posy as you work and check to make sure you are creating a domed effect. When complete, trim wire stems and bind with stem binding tape. Cover handle with ribbon (page 23)

◄ A highly original candle arrangement which would make a spectacular decoration for a New Year celebration.

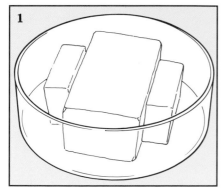

1 Place blocks of foam into dish leaving approximately a 2.5cm (1in) margin in which to fit the nuts and moss.

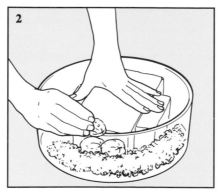

2 Place nuts and moss around foam both to hold foam in place and to look attractive.

3 Tape cane pieces to bottom of candles (page 19) and place 1cm ($^1/_2$in) apart. In order, add hawthorn, fruits, cinnamon. Pin chilli string to foam.

1 Set the branch in a bowl using nylon-reinforced plaster (page 22). Cover top of plaster with moss.

2 Trim the ends of oblong pieces of foam at an angle and glue together to form a large oblong oval shape. Mount onto branch. (Page 22) Cut fruits from original stems leaving as much stem as possible. Wire large fruits singly with 18 gauge wires; smaller fruits in small and large bunches. Cover all wires with stem binding tape. Position fruits close together in foam. Intersperse the leaves.

◀ A chunky topiary of plump artificial fruits makes a colourful centrepiece.

Managing Editor: Jo Finnis
Editor: Sue Wilkinson
Design: Art of Design
Photography: Steve Tanner
Production: Ruth Arthur; Sally Connolly; Neil Randles;
Karen Staff; Matthew Dale; Jonathan Tickner
Production Director: Gerald Hughes

DEDICATION
To my wonderful children Olivia and Clarence
who make everything worthwhile.